The
RIVER

Seeing God and Walking
in the Miracle

NICHOLAS BRANCH

THE RIVER

Seeing God and Walking in the Miracle

Copyright © 2024 – Nicholas Branch

All rights reserved.

Author photo by Ethan Lopez, Wolfmedia.ltd

Printed in the United States of America

Dedication

I dedicate this book first to You Lord. You who gave man his mouth. You loved me before I ever existed. You sacrificed yourself for my sins. The miraculous is your every day. You are so good and so great. It is difficult to remember each day. Thank you for in your greatness, you also weep beside me in my grief. That in your goodness, all things that do not belong to me you wipe away as many times as it takes. Holy, Holy, Holy is your name. Thank you for being my wing-man and best friend now and for the rest of my days by your grace.

I dedicate it also to you, Heidi, my love. Your beauty and kindness know no limits as it flows from our Father. You are a powerful, worthy, and abundant woman. I am honored to share space with you and grow in the Lord next to you. I love visualizations of what God has for us together. Thank you for creating, imagining, cleaning off, talking through, and just plain loving me the way you do. I pray I cherish you all the days of our lives as the precious gift you are.

I dedicate this also to my three children Carina, Niko, and Lilli. I thought of you when I didn't even know who you were at six. You are so precious to me. I love you more than you can imagine. God loves you even more than that. I'm proud each of you, in your unique beautiful ways, that you get to be such a gift to this earth.

I dedicate this to my mother, who sacrificed everything to make sure her children succeeded. Who made magic happen in my eyes as a child.

Everything we wanted even if it made no sense how it could happen. Impeccable character and such a high standard you set for all of us. I'm blessed God made you the mother I got to live life honoring. With a stepdad, who is a man I love and respect so much.

I dedicate this to my father, who has created a beautiful life for himself and all around him. Who kept walking into better versions of himself. Who came from a loving space, an amazing teacher, and a loving father/grandfather. I'm blessed God choose you as my father that I got to go through life with.

And to all my family, loved ones, and friends. I love you so dearly, thank you for being a part of my life it is an honor to be with you.

Contents

CHAPTER 1

LOVE

I was three years old, a bold and curious little boy.

We joke about it now, but by then, I had already driven a van and a car—a life full of early adventures. I remember grabbing a baseball bat and chasing my older half-sister around our home.

I talked all the time, never afraid to share my opinion, always fearless and bold.

I vividly recall sneaking upstairs at my Grandma's home in Philadelphia to see my Grandpa, who was bedridden after a stroke. My mom often said I resembled him in many ways. We were supposed to leave him alone, but I was too adventurous and curious.

I still remember the love and joy in his eyes, even though he couldn't move, as he became a "captive audience" for everything I wanted to tell him. His World War II uniform and security guard uniform, each with a stylish police-style cap, were proudly displayed in my grandmother's basement.

I can still smell the wood cabinet where those uniforms were kept.

I loved playing soldier or officer with his caps. Later in life, one of my older male cousins—yes, there were far more women in the great family home my grandmother built—suggested I need to earn one that uniform. That suggestion had a profound impact on my life.

Now, about those unexpected driving lessons—those are likely my earliest memories, probably because of the shock they caused my parents.

On one particular occasion, my dad made a quick stop at the store. The store was on a slight hill, so he put the car in park and engaged the parking brake.

I remember feeling so curious and bold, sitting in the back seat of my dad's vehicle. I had watched, unnoticed, every time my parents got in and out of the car. I'd seen them put the car in park and shift into drive. I thought, "I know how to drive!"

I can't count the times in my life that I've watched something and thought I was an expert. That mindset must've set in early on.

In the peak of my boldness and excitement, I couldn't stay in my seat. I unbuckled my seatbelt and jumped right into the front seat. The joy was like going on a fast ride. I used to cry whenever my dad slowed down for a stop sign or red light. It felt like being picked up to fly around in the air with my Poppop.

I put my hands on the steering wheel, standing in the driver's seat, ready to drive around the block and come back to pick up my dad. I turned the wheel back and forth, just like it was a race car. I could feel all the nooks and crannies in the steering wheel meant to enhance grip.

I forgot something: the parking brake. I couldn't go anywhere unless I released it. Like a big person, I popped that brake right off and started to go.

As the van rolled down the hill, I felt the movement. The van was slowly moving forward, just as I'd hoped. I was really moving now, turning the steering wheel back and forth even more vigorously.

2

My dad rushed back out to stop the van before anything catastrophic could happen. The store clerk was shocked by what had happened and even offered my dad "a drink," saying he needed it.

When my dad called my mom to tell her what happened, she responded with, "Again?!" I vaguely remember this one, but I do recall my first test run in my mom's little car.

These stories live on during family gatherings, and my children have heard them several times. It's beautiful.

I was such a bold, fearless, and social little boy, full of wonder at all life had to offer. Curious about everything, smiling at every opportunity, and loving every embrace, I'd tease or prank the older children in my family. I was pure joy, hating to slow down, always wanting to have fun.

My beautiful qualities were not yet tainted by the world around me. Boldness—if something could be done or was possible, I stepped into it. It's a trait I've come to love and accept in myself again. It feels like a lost pet that has finally come back to me.

We had a cat named Jinx, after a popular cat and mouse cartoon. He was my best friend—bold like me.

Ever heard of a cat that loved water? Well, this one did. He would jump into the bathtub with me every night. I'd sit in the warm, calming waters, playing with my bath toys, my imagination running wild as I pretended to be on the open seas.

The tub felt like a pool or a lake, and I'd wave my hands back and forth to create waves like the ocean. Even at that tender age, I was already dreaming of navigating the seas and waters of the world.

My parents, of course, wanted to keep the apartment clean, not have a wet cat walking, climbing, and jumping on everything. They tried to stop Jinx as he crouched down like a kid getting ready to do a cannonball into a pool. I'd turn around just in time to see him, my face lighting up with a big smile. "Come on in, you can do it!" I'd cheer.

And with a big splash, Jinx would defy the odds—a house cat that loved water.

Even if he wasn't supposed to, Jinx didn't hold back, jumping fully into what he wanted to do. I loved him and his boldness, snuggling him every chance I got, pulling him into my adventures.

We eventually had to give him away because I developed allergies to cats. In my mind, I thought he'd jumped into the tub a few too many times. I still remember the sadness of losing my first friend when he didn't come back home.

I was loved—I could feel it all around me, and I gave love freely, as if it were natural to let it flow in and out of me. I can still feel it now, stepping back into this bold trust of receiving and giving love, like a long embrace where the vibrations of love pass between two people as they hold each other.

My concept and feeling of love felt pure back then.

One night, I overheard my parents arguing loudly, enough to wake me up. This wasn't the first time they argued. Something was different this time. I could feel it in the air. I felt scared to take a step—the bold boy unafraid to drive a car was frozen in his tracks, my heart afraid to see what was happening.

But something moved me forward, despite the vicious yelling and screaming. The smell of blood—a scent I would become familiar with from watching samurai movies and anime when I was older—hung in the air in this house of love.

I stepped out and saw my mom and dad fighting violently. My mom looked intent on hurting him.

And she could—my mom is a small, powerful woman. I remember our German Shepherd mix, when I was a teenager, cowering and peeing in fear whenever she walked in.

She didn't have to say anything or raise a hand—your very being knew this was a powerful presence. I've met very few people who match that kind of aura. She had her sights set on my dad, her husband. Like a lioness, there was ferocity in her eyes.

Blood was coming from my dad's arm, and he wasn't holding back either. They threw each other around, against the wall, over the coffee table. Maybe it was glass or her fingernails—my mom had something sharp, and I saw blood all around.

I stood there in cold fear, crying, hoping they would stop if they saw or heard me. They didn't.

The two people who loved each other enough to create me were set on hurting each other. No matter how I cried or positioned myself, I couldn't stop it.

Two people I loved, who were supposed to love each other, seemed to hate each other. I couldn't understand why. Maybe someone "deserved" it. All I saw and felt was anger, rage, and malice.

When I was older, my stepdad would wonder why I was much quieter than the rest of my family. This memory always came to mind. I never told anyone until I was in my twenties.

I distinctly remember this as the point when I changed completely, at about four years old. It felt like a hand was around my throat, holding back my voice. I was no longer fearless but filled with fear.

I was scared to use my voice; the wildly curious, joyful little boy was gone, and in his place was someone shaped by what I had just witnessed.

CHAPTER 2

LOST

My parents divorced shortly afterward. It was just my mom, my two little sisters, and me after it became clear that reconciliation between my parents was impossible.

My youngest sister was less than a year old, maybe around six months. I don't know exactly how much time passed. This was the most painful period of my life, and I felt an overwhelming sense of sorrow.

Broken bones, torn muscles, shoulder injuries, concussions—I wouldn't experience pain like I felt at this time. Friends and family often marveled at how I never seemed to feel pain, almost admiring me for this strange trait.

I never acknowledged pain, a tendency that served me well in sports and during military service, pushing me to complete challenges I might not have otherwise managed.

None of those physical injuries compared to the emotional wounds I refused to process or even admit were there. Wounds that would lead me to the lowest points of my life.

As a man who has now gone through a divorce myself—something neither my ex-wife nor I wanted—I see divorce differently. This is my story of that time in my life.

We moved from our apartment just outside the city in Philly back to my grandma's house in West Philly. The four of us—my mom and her three children—crowded into that small space. I remember my kindergarten graduation, but not much else.

My dad had been absent for some time; I'm sure my parents were trying to work things out. I don't recall seeing him at all during that period.

It could have been a year or two; it felt like something in between. I chose to forget most of what happened during that time, except for a few vivid memories.

My mom, with the support of my grandmother, continued to work, trying to make ends meet while also attempting to reconcile with my dad.

She arranged for him to pick us up on Friday afternoons to spend time with us—my two sisters and me. We would sit on my grandmother's blue couch, which had a plastic cover to keep it clean. It squeaked every time you moved on it.

We waited, excited because we were told that Daddy was coming. Grandma helped us get ready.

I was going to see my dad—how was he doing? What silly moves would he do to make us laugh? These thoughts raced through my mind as we moved outside to the stone steps in front of my grandma's row home.

The ground was cold, and we had to behave and sit still. I held my baby sister while my younger sister sat beside me. We waited, but he never came. Disappointed, we gathered our things and went back inside.

The next Friday, the same routine. My mom worked her hardest, and Grandma got us ready. Holding my baby sister, with my little sister next to me, we waited. Again, he didn't show. We gathered our things and went back inside.

This became our reality for months, maybe close to a year. I chose to stop feeling excited. I started imagining that my dad was in one of the cars that drove by, counting each one, hoping every single time that it would be him.

"He said he was coming," I thought, "so he must be in that car." I convinced myself that he saw us sitting on the steps and decided not to stop, just kept driving.

I would tell my sisters, "We need to sit up straight, look ahead, fix our clothes, and be good so Daddy wouldn't drive by this time while we waited."

We had to look perfect for him so he would want to pick us up. This was the story I created—a story that made the most sense to a child desperate for love.

"I have to be perfect to be loved." An untruth I am still actively dismantling.

Later in life, I would dream about this time. I used to be disgusted by the sight of that boy—hoping with all his heart to be picked up. Every Friday, like a new Friday, brought hope for the only thing I wanted at that time.

Pathetic, pitiful, disgusting—who would want to pick this boy up? So, I sat taller, made sure my sister was sitting perfectly still, rocked my baby sister so she wouldn't cry, hoping he would say, "Okay, I'll stop and pick them up."

It didn't happen. Months went by, and I would relive this experience many times in the future—hoping, and then nothing.

One Friday, there was so much self-hate in me that it was toxic. I didn't know what I was doing this time, but I heard once more that Daddy was coming to pick us up. I believed again because it was all I could do—hope, one more time.

I can still feel the squeaking plastic cover on that blue couch as my grandma told us our dad was coming.

We moved to the steps, prepared as usual. I straightened up, but this time, I didn't tell my sisters to sit still or stop playing. I just stared at the road. He never came.

We waited longer than ever before—if this was a test of endurance, I was determined to pass with whatever strength I had left. I sat still, waiting until my mom got home. My last hope, and he never came.

This time, I felt like I was just taking up space, like I didn't belong on this earth. I caved into myself, sinking into a numbness like never before.

My mother was furious. I was numb. She rushed us back inside. We stood around that blue couch with the plastic cover, and she called my dad. We sat on the couch and waited.

She got ahold of him, argued for a while, and then told him to at least speak to his son. She gestured for me to come over.

I got up, feeling pathetic, worthless, yet still hopeful one more time. A mix of desperate hope and a sense of not deserving to be there wrapped around me.

My mother handed me the corded phone, heavy in my hands. All I could think about was how desperate I was to hear my dad's voice. My dad, who took us to the movies, who made funny faces to make us laugh, who took us to the park, who made us dinner, who loved us.

What could I say to bring him back, to make him see that I loved him?

In my absolute desperation, all I could manage to say was, "I love you."

Desperate, desperate—the very definition of desperation. Remembering this made me feel disgusted in my twenties. I hated that boy, hated myself for so many years—desperately clinging to hope, to someone.

The sound of the phone hanging up felt like death. It felt like I died in that moment. I held the phone receiver as if I had just pulled the sword from my own body that killed me, staring down at it.

The dial tone droned in the background.

But I lived.

This was the lowest, most worthless I have ever felt in my life.

My mother saw me holding the phone and rushed over. "What happened?!" she asked.

I whispered, as I would continue to do through much of my life after that point, "He hung up."

My mom was angrier and more hurt than I had ever seen her.

I just remember the words "full custody." I didn't know what they meant, but I felt it. She was never going to give my dad another chance, and I would never see him again.

Feeling half-dead, I pulled hope from somewhere deep inside me, somewhere I didn't know existed. I begged my mom not to do it, not to take whatever action she was considering, not to take away another chance from my dad.

I cried and begged her, desperate—so desperate. These memories, half-repressed, would haunt me well into my twenties.

I became afraid to say "I love you" to anyone. So many people reached out first to say those words to me, and I was so gripped by fear that I couldn't speak, even though I knew I loved them—my family, my best friends.

I became afraid of hanging up the phone on my own children, terrified that I might accidentally hang up on them before they could say "I love you."

I was also resilient. The quality I chose to hold on to from that boy was his forgiving heart, without judgment, in that moment.

Months passed before I would see my dad again. I do not remember much of the time in between, but the next day I saw him changed my entire world.

CHAPTER 3

DROWNING

I remember the awkward sensation that day, the numbness that replaced the hope I once felt about seeing my dad.

After that last time, I stopped wishing he would show up. When I found out we were going to see him again, I was guarded, as if I'd built a ten-layer wall around myself for protection.

The pain from that last disappointment was so overwhelming that I could barely move through the world. I felt as if I could be blown away at any moment, merely going through the motions at six and a half years old.

We moved a couple times, shifting schools until we eventually settled into the house where my mom would raise my sisters and me. During that time, I struggled to make friends.

In fact, after kindergarten until I started second grade, I remember little else besides the pain. I was extremely quiet, considered smart but socially awkward when it came to making friends.

I often felt worthless, wondering, "Who would want to be friends with me?" I was just taking up space. My mom was busy trying to make ends meet—I wondered if she even noticed.

And then came the day—the day I would actually see my dad for the first time in what felt like forever.

My baby sister was one, and my younger sister was a little over four, as far as I can recall. My dad lived in an apartment on a steep cement hill in Philly.

I didn't have any expectations or excitement—I just existed. It felt like hugging someone who doesn't feel worthy of the hug, someone who has nothing to give back. That's what it felt like to have my dad there for the first time.

Before the divorce, my dad used to cook a lot and take us places. He was called "Mr. Mom" or something like that. He had been out of practice. It was obvious that day that I wasn't the only one trying to figure out what our relationship looked like now.

My baby sister had a huge diaper bag filled with all her necessities, and my younger sister and I each had our own bags with everything we'd need. My mom always made sure we were prepared—that was one of her strengths.

My dad was determined to take us to the park. As a father now, I understand the feeling of sticking to a plan—going to the park or the movies—no matter what. Especially when you don't get to see your children every day.

No matter what came.

Dad attempted to carry all our stuff for the picnic, including our bags. It wasn't working. He handed me a bag, and my younger sister a bag, while he managed the rest along with our baby sister.

I remember feeling like our load was too heavy, but once an adult gives you something to carry, you'd better not complain. I was certainly not in a state of mind to complain—I accepted whatever came.

As we started walking down the big cement hill, my younger sister, carrying the large diaper bag, got her foot tangled in it. The bag was almost her size, and as soon as she planted her foot again, it pulled her down.

She tumbled at least fifty feet down the cement hill.

Her face was covered in scrapes and blood, and all of us were in shock. She began to cry and scream—it looked so painful.

"Should we go to the hospital? Should we go back to Mommy?" Those were the thoughts running through our minds.

What did this look like to the people walking by? My dad helped blot her face. We were still going to the park.

I was scared—her face was scraped up and bleeding badly. Was she going to be okay? We were still going to the park.

Our baby sister seemed blissfully unaware of what was happening. My younger sister kept crying in pain, and I, too scared to take a stand, couldn't really look at my dad. We got in the car, and my dad packed everything away. My sister had a towel over her face, trying to breathe as the blood slowly stopped.

We drove to the river drive along the Schuylkill River in Philadelphia. I wasn't sure if we should be there—shouldn't we be at the hospital? My sister didn't look well. That feeling you get as a kid when you really don't want to be somewhere, but an adult tells you to be grateful for being there—that's what I felt as we got out of the car and prepared for our picnic.

Dad carefully laid out the picnic blanket and made a spot for my sister to rest. She had stopped crying but was still breathing heavily. He held our baby sister, making sure she was safe, and laid out everything for the day.

I still had a bit of the explorer in me and saw that my dad was occupied with my sisters. He was attending to their every need—the loving dad I remembered.

I felt comfortable enough to wander a bit, and one thing I loved searching for was a stick that looked like a sword.

The idea of a Japanese katana, like in a samurai show, or a regal knight's sword serving his king, was my favorite. I imagined myself as my favorite cartoon heroes who wielded swords for justice.

For many years, I felt like I should have been born during the warring states period as a samurai in Japan or a mighty warrior who brought peace to the land, serving with honor and integrity.

Even at that age, a sword meant something to me. It represented something I felt I couldn't be further from. If I could find a sword, I could retreat into my imagination and play while my dad took care of my sisters.

I looked around carefully and quietly. I had in mind exactly what the sword would look like, and then I saw it. It was a few feet down a little hill leading towards the water. The park was green and beautiful, with a sunny sky overhead. It was a beautiful place to be, right next to the river—however dirty the river might have been.

Apparently, it had rained the night before because there was some mud in the area. I spotted the stick—it looked just like a long sword from the samurai shows I watched. That sword was for me.

I slipped a couple of times as the hill was much muddier than I expected. "If I just move slower and balance with my hands out, I can get to it," I thought.

"What's the worst that could happen?" I wondered. Maybe I'd fall. As I got closer, I realized it was all mud, and looking down the hill, I saw nothing but mud. This was more dangerous than I had thought.

In that state of mind, I needed that sword. I needed validation— maybe it would give me courage. Maybe I could save lives and be a hero.

Maybe I could do something with it to prove I was worth taking up space on this earth.

Maybe my dad would be proud of me.

Maybe I could hold something in my hand with honor and not be disgusted with myself.

I reached the sword, and in a moment of joy, I stood up from my crouched position, so happy to have reached it despite the challenge.

Then everything was pulled out from under me.

I slipped and fell, sliding down the muddy path so fast I couldn't grab onto anything to slow down. The sword was gone—I was holding on for dear life. It was like a water slide, but with terror and death waiting at the bottom.

I tried to move or roll to either side, but it was so slick, and I was moving so fast that my reactions were pointless.

I was thrown into the river.

It had rained a lot, which is probably why it was so muddy, and the river was full and raging.

I didn't know how to swim, and as powerful as the river was, I wonder if it would have made any difference even if I did.

The terror of landing in that water was something I would never experience again physically. I would feel it emotionally many times in my life.

As soon as I hit the river, I was swept away. I was a skinny kid, so it didn't take much to push me around.

Survival instincts kicked in. I knew I couldn't swim, but this was literally life or death. Don't people talk about finding strength out of nowhere, like dogs instinctively knowing how to swim to survive?

To this day, I cringe when people say things like that. When someone asks what you would do in a life-or-death situation, and they confidently say, "We're stronger than we know."

I immediately started strategizing. First: could survival instincts kick in and teach me to swim? I tried to dog paddle, tried to freestyle based on what I'd seen. The river was unforgiving. It grabbed my head and slammed me under the water twice, tossing my body around like a rag doll.

That didn't work. "Come on, you might not have many friends, but you're really smart—everyone says so," I told myself. Next strategy: could I get close enough to the shore to grab onto the tree roots and stop my forward momentum?

I grasped and grasped, trying to position my body with all my strength to get closer to the shore. I was going too fast, too forcefully.

The unforgiving river submerged me twice more, tossing my head and body around, flipping me in the water as my body started to fill with water.

I won't survive if this keeps happening. I had to think of another strategy.

The river was dirty and muddy, filled with trash and debris. When I was underwater, I couldn't tell where I was.

Last strategy: Thanks to the amount of dirt and trash in the river, there was a sort of mud-and-trash island in the middle of the river

18

further downstream. If I let the river carry me toward it, maybe I could make it to that island and wait to be rescued.

Then a new wave of alarm hit me as I was pushed further down the river. The parkland was coming to an end, and the river was opening up to where the highway starts. If I didn't do something, any chance of getting to the island or the shore would be gone. And I'd be dead.

I tried to scoot to the left, to get further in, but the river body-slammed me again, and I felt my eyes starting to close—I was blacking out. The island was out of reach, and I could see the land ending. I went under again, my body filling with water, tossed around with no control.

No one knew what was happening—I hadn't screamed or yelled for help. As I write this, I'm crying, even today, because I tried to save myself from death.

I didn't want to bother anyone to come help me, even though my life depended on it.

My dad, lovingly taking care of my sisters, had no idea. All he knew was that I had wandered off and would be back for lunch.

I couldn't even muster a scream to save my life. That was where I had chosen to believe that my life wasn't worth anyone's effort to save.

Too many times would I come back to this thought process in my life.

As I was being tossed around, seeing the dirt island out of reach and the inevitable approach of death as the river opened up by the highway, I saw no way out. My life flashed before my eyes.

The bloody night when my mom and dad fought. The pitiful little boy waiting on the steps, sitting so still he wouldn't move for fear that if he made the slightest mistake or slouched even an inch, his father would drive away. The boy holding his little sisters. The boy who held the phone receiver in his hand after experiencing the worst feeling imaginable after he desperately confessed his love.

What a life. How worthless of a life. What was worth living another second? I resigned myself to giving up at that moment.

My prayer: "From Sunday school, God, I know You don't make mistakes. But just this once, You can take the eraser side of the pencil and erase me. I didn't need to exist—everyone will be happy. My parents—maybe they'll love each other again. I don't have to have ever existed anywhere."

CHAPTER 4

LAST BREATH

I went under again, my body no longer resisting, surrendering to what I believed was my fate: to be erased by the God of all heaven and earth.

To have never existed.

As I slipped in and out of consciousness, I had only two regrets.

The first was that I would never find someone who would love me for who I was. Someone with whom I could be myself, and they would accept me. Someone who would stay by my side and never leave, with whom I could share my life.

A person who would love me, all of me, just as I am, without needing to perform or prove anything. In that moment, it was a woman—a wife and life partner—that I thought of, and I wasn't even seven years old.

The second regret was that I would never have the blessing of children. I longed to pass on a part of myself, to be a father, to give my love and hold my children close.

I wouldn't be able to raise them, snuggle them, and shower them with all the love I had to give.

Those were my only regrets. People often like to say what we will or won't regret in our last moments.

"You'll regret not spending more time with your family, instead of going to the office."

"You'll regret not taking that leap, asking her out, trying out for that team, or jumping into that opportunity."

We all have opinions on what we may or may not regret as we approach our final hour.

My question to anyone reading this is: Do you know what you would regret in your last breath?

As my body twisted to the side and went under one last time, I closed my eyes, resigned to the thought of never existing—neither on earth nor in heaven. I took what I believed would be my last breath.

CHAPTER 5

GLORY

I found myself standing on what felt like solid land, my frail frame perched on a hill. As my eyes slowly opened, the colors around me were unlike anything I had ever seen.

Everything seemed to have a purple-maroon hue—the most regal color I'd ever encountered, a shade beyond description. There was a golden light, deeper and richer than any I'd known, as if the colors themselves were alive and pulsing.

This golden light permeated every part of the ground, almost as if it were nourishing the earth itself, like a stream of water or a path of light flowing through the soil.

The grass was green, but not like any green I'd seen before. It was alive, pulsing and flowing with a richness that felt like pure life. It didn't seem to belong to the normal color spectrum. Somehow, I was standing on this ground, even though just a moment ago, I was underwater, taking what I thought would be my last breath.

The best way I can describe it is that this felt like a mirror dimension to where I had been moments before—River Drive at the park by the Schuylkill River. In this place, the colors were alive, vibrant in a way I had never seen and would never see again.

As I became aware that I was standing, I felt a weight in this place. The best comparison I can think of is from later in life when I watched *Dragon Ball Z*, where the characters trained at different gravity levels. It felt like the gravity here was several times that of the earth I had just left. And yet, I could stand in this place.

I had no idea where I was or what was happening. I had just resigned myself to never exist. I was confused, having reached the bottom of my being, only to find myself in a place I didn't know or understand.

But love—love and light—pulsed through the very essence of this place. I felt cradled, supported by the light that filled everything.

There were trees here, different from the ones at the park, yet somehow familiar. They were the most beautiful, wise trees, with leaves that shimmered, moved, and vibrated with life in a way I had never experienced on earth. The grass and leaves seemed to dance in joyous movement.

My eyes were fixed at waist level and below, a physical manifestation of the low part of my heart as I entered death. I couldn't look up; it felt as if my head were too heavy to raise.

I stood there, head down, as if I were disappointed to have existed somewhere—as if I had been given another chance only to be a disappointment once again. This downward gaze was a position I had grown familiar with over the past two years and would take years more to overcome.

Then, someone of immeasurable power and love appeared before me, unlike anything I had ever experienced. Words cannot describe the beautiful tapestry of infinite power and unconditional love woven into one being.

He stood in front of me, and it felt as though I could be crushed by this power at any moment. Yet, that power gave me the strength to stand before Him.

It supported me, held my body together, healed me, and warmed me in a way I had never experienced before and would never experience again.

My eyes, feeling the weight of His presence, slowly lifted from waist level, rising to His chest, then His neck. As they grew heavier, the light strengthened me. Eyes that could no longer look people in the eye before I died were now moving upward toward His face.

When my eyes reached His shoulders and then His face, I noticed something behind Him—a sun, infinitely brighter than our own, yet I could look at it directly.

It was the source of all light and power in this place. I don't know how I understood this, but I knew it in that instant.

The light, more powerful than the sun, seemed to be right next to the man and in the sky far above at the same time. I've never seen anything like it—it was near and far simultaneously, beyond what our dimensional space can describe.

His eyes were like the light—connected, one and the same. I couldn't comprehend or do justice to the power this central light and His eyes held.

At my lowest, feeling broken and worthless, those eyes and that light loved me more than I could ever describe. In their power, they saw me— not with pity, shame, or disappointment, but with pure love.

My self-pity and feelings of worthlessness were blown away. My eyes felt unworthy of this gaze. I think now, as I remember, it was almost like

Simon Peter asking the Lord to go away from him because he was a sinful man.

I had just asked God to erase me, to take away my existence, and now here I was, being loved and regarded as if I mattered so much to these two.

As if I were important, precious. They didn't need to say anything; as much as I wanted to hide in my self-pity, their love poured into me.

Then the light, more powerful than the sun, spoke. It reverberated everywhere—through the ground, the sky, the air, my thoughts, my body, my cells, my mind. It was the most powerful sensation I have ever felt or would ever feel in my life.

He spoke, affirming that it was not my time to leave this world and that I would change the world.

In the most loving way, the man I believed was Jesus, whose eyes were like that light, did not look away from me. His eyes reassured me, without an ounce of pity or doubt. He believed the words I had just received.

Honestly, I had just drowned, given up on life, and made peace with not existing, so I was in shock—I just stood there.

I was still trembling from everything that had happened, but I felt the deepest love I had ever known.

In that moment, God gave me purpose. He loved me and held me through every atom in that dimension without physically touching me, as we know it in the normal world. Everything in that place, powered by His light and love, wrapped around me.

He spoke with a confidence that our word for confidence cannot capture. His power and will are beyond human understanding.

What I felt in that moment, I write about now, though for most of my life, I thought I would never share this experience.

And here I am, trying to describe the indescribable.

The eyes of our Lord Jesus, the light of the most sovereign God, looked upon me with such love and belief in me—such reassurance.

Unconditional love has a different depth and meaning as I recount this experience.

I believe our Lord speaks these reassurances and messages over us all the time. How do you receive His love, His reassurance, His words of affirmation?

I noticed figures in the background, looking on. They were at a distance, around the trees—shapes of humans, maybe ten or so.

They appeared more like shadows, and it wasn't for me to know who they were. I did notice that I was not alone. It wasn't just Jesus and our Lord there.

The very next thing I knew, I opened my eyes to the familiar colors of this world.

I found my right hand gripping the root of a tree that extended over the water.

My hand held firmly onto the root, suspending me just above the water. The beauty of that tree, extending its root out over the water to receive its nutrients—God had placed me back on earth, holding onto that root.

It's unexplainable by human standards, and yet, I lived it.

I, who had resigned myself to non-existence, was back, hanging by the root of a tree over the water.

There's so much depth to that—my last name, Branch, the tree extending its roots to the water to sustain life, also doing the work of the Lord to be there as my support.

I placed my left hand on the root and began pulling myself toward the tree and the land, covered in mud, soaking wet, and somehow, alive.

CHAPTER 6

THE TWIST

What just happened?

I stumbled and walked up the hill to the grassy area, dazed and confused. I didn't descend like Moses, with clarity or purpose—I looked like a kid who had just jumped into a dirty river, soaking wet, disoriented, and searching for my dad and sisters.

In that moment, I was simply shocked by everything that had transpired.

I finally stumbled over to my dad, who saw me muddy and drenched. He ran over as I approached, where he was caring for my sisters—my younger sister lying on the blanket, her face still covered but no longer bleeding, just resting, while my baby sister carried on with her little world.

"What happened to you?!" he exclaimed, scared and shocked.

All I could mutter was, "I fell in the river," and then I started crying as he grabbed me and laid me down on the blanket.

I didn't mention anything about God, Jesus, dying, or the miraculous experience I had just gone through. I wonder now why I didn't speak of it.

Was it that, even at six years old, I knew it was unbelievable?

Was I in too much shock?

Something made it harder to speak that truth in the moment.

I was already struggling to talk with my dad after our last conversation, so maybe I just didn't have the words.

I wouldn't speak about this experience for decades, and even then, only in pieces.

My dad had one infant-toddler, one daughter whose face was covered in blood, and a son who had just fallen into the river.

It was his first time back in our lives, and he was determined to make sure we had a beautiful day at the park by the river.

He didn't give up; he kept showing up. By all rights, that could have been the worst day a father could imagine. But by the grace of God, he held us in His hands.

As high as the heavens are above the earth, so are the ways of our loving God beyond ours.

You can imagine what awaited him when he brought us home to my mother. As we walked up to the door, my mother looked at her children—it was a miracle she allowed us to see him again.

The story that was passed down in our family was that he had jumped in and saved me.

But how do we process the impossible, the miraculous, when it happens right in front of us?

It wasn't earned, and it challenges the "Just World" hypothesis and all that comes with it.

How do we process the miraculous?

It's a question I need to remind myself of when I witness a miracle and either sweep it under the rug or take credit for what God has done for me.

That's not the twist I reference in the title of this chapter.

There is no one that got away. Everything good that God has for us is in front of us. I have no regrets about staying silent for so long on this experience, but eventually, fear set in.

What would people think?

How would my dad react?

No one will believe me, so why share it anyway?

These are all the voices of fear, the language that does not come from God. They're akin to shame, blame, hate, and guilt.

The enemy, the adversary, the accuser—Satan, or whatever name you choose for the evil force in this world—this is where that language originates.

From the very first sin, evil has twisted the words of God, starting with a manipulative question rooted in the fear that God might be holding something back.

Where in our lives are we letting the voice of fear twist the words of truth?

Allowing the enemy's two goals to occur: separating us from God and separating us from each other.

I stood in fear of what my dad might think, what other people might think, and the thought that I could be so special in God's eyes as to receive such a gift.

I wasn't glowing from an unbelievable experience, or boldly stepping into life with a second chance, living on the edge as we often hear from others who've had near-death experiences.

Instead, I chose to shrink into fear, letting the voice of the enemy twist the most beautiful words and love I would ever experience into pressure.

In my spirit, it sounded like this: "You need to change the world," as if it were a task I didn't feel up to.

This misrepresentation of God's word led me to live for decades feeling like I was disappointing Him and every authority figure in my life.

First, I had to face myself on the other side of a miracle.

CHAPTER 7

THE MIRROR

The memory of the river eventually faded, and I returned to my normal life.

I was still pretty awkward, adjusting to life in a different part of Philly. I chose to remain in fear, uncertain of the next steps I needed to take—living in a new area, attending a new school, and for the first time since the divorce, thinking about making friends.

There was a deep self-hatred within me, something that would take a lifetime to overcome through healing and learning to love myself.

But first, I had to look in the mirror.

There was a saying I remembered from growing up: "Don't look in the mirror too long, or you'll become vain." The idea was that staring at yourself for too long would make you conceited.

I'm not sure where this myth, old saying, or bit of "wisdom" came from. It was ingrained in me.

In that moment, feeling worthless, I knew I had to do something to move forward.

I had a "second chance," that much was undeniable.

But I didn't live my life, and still don't, with the reckless abandon or hyper-spirituality I often associate with someone who's been given a second chance.

I chose instead to take the next best step forward—nothing grand, glamorous, or inspiring.

I knew I needed to build more confidence. But I could still feel the lingering sense of worthlessness.

I was good at math and reasoning. My logical mind pieced together a plan.

I envisioned a fictional confidence spectrum, with one end representing the lack of self-worth I was starting from, and the other end representing conceit (which, to my analytical mind, was an excess of confidence).

It clicked in my head what my next step had to be.

At seven years old, I reasoned that if I looked at myself in the mirror a little bit each day, I could gradually increase my confidence.

Fragile and frail reasoning. It was the best I had.

So, I did it.

I still remember the pain and disgust I felt looking at myself in the mirror that first time. I couldn't hold my gaze for more than a second— there was so much pity, hate, and disdain for the person I saw.

My eyes immediately darted back down to waist level.

Every day, I forced myself to look as long as I could bear it.

I saw everything about myself as imperfect, as trash. I kept looking.

One second, then two, then three. It brings me to tears to think of how many of us carry this level of pain when looking at ourselves.

At the same time, I continued seeking approval from others and was extremely sensitive to feedback.

I remember, before I knew how to iron shirts, wearing a wrinkled shirt.

I wouldn't have noticed, as I still couldn't look hard enough in the mirror to care about my clothes.

I went over to my dad's house, and he was displeased that I had left the house looking disheveled. He let me know it. He cared about my appearance more than I did.

All I heard was his displeasure: "Don't come out of the house like that again."

The attachment to people-pleasing that had set in was so heavy, and I let it grip me well into my thirties.

After that, I wouldn't leave home without ironing until every wrinkle was gone. I immediately demanded that my mom teach me how to iron and where the iron was kept.

This desperate need to look perfect so I would be accepted and loved reached its extreme when I once missed an entire event with my college friends. I spent two hours ironing my clothes to get every wrinkle out.

I was so desperate to be seen.

I believed I had to be perfect, or I would be rejected.

These false thoughts swirled around me unnoticed for most of my life.

It wasn't until I was a teenager that I could look at myself in the mirror long enough to hold a gaze.

And decades later, I would eventually learn that it's okay to want to look sharp or fresh, but I had to ask: Where is that desire coming from?

Is it from the fear of not being loved or accepted?

Fear that leads to pride in one's appearance?

Or is it coming from love—the love of God, knowing that I am wonderfully made, and the love of myself as I am?

Thankfully, God has been dedicated to dismantling my pride and arrogance over the years, continually working on me to reveal the most beautiful parts of myself.

As I started meeting new friends and connecting with more people in the neighborhood, I found other ways to gain acceptance. I was athletic and pretty tough, which made it easier to be accepted in sports.

I began learning how to dress to impress, perform on the court, field, or blacktop, and excel in the classroom—all in a bid to gain acceptance.

CHAPTER 8

PRESSURE

It would take decades—and the love of the beautiful woman God promised to bring into my life—for me to realize what I had done with God's words in Chapter 6.

The subtle twist of the enemy had turned those words of ultimate affirmation into pressure.

The weight of performance and the need to meet everyone's expectations settled in. It grabbed hold of my chest and wouldn't let go.

It felt like every expectation was a rock that people placed on my chest. Before I knew it, it looked like one of those carefully balanced piles of stones you see on the beach, where each person adds another rock to see how high it can get.

Except under that pile of rocks, carefully and lovingly placed, was the chest of a boy trying to breathe. Trying to feel worthy of the breath he just took.

One of my favorite movies features a main character who draws graffiti art underground, visualizing the pressure of everyone's expectations and the trap that can create.

That's exactly what it felt like for me, from my teenage years into adulthood.

It was as if an external binder was keeping my very being restrained. Tightening around my body. A heart-wrenching pressure in my chest that never let go. As long as I sought approval, I could get temporary relief when I achieved "success."

I went from being picked last to one of the first picked. I falsely placed my hopes and self-worth in the hands of whoever was choosing the teams.

Is this the time I don't get picked?

Will everyone playing ball realize I'm not good enough?

Will I not be accepted?

I had to get better; I had to be perfect.

I had to catch every pass, make every shot on the blacktop.

As if my life depended on it.

As if my connection with other people depended on it.

Job searches, making teams, winning awards at school—all these things became measures of my worth, driven by the fear that I wouldn't be accepted or loved.

The feeling of success was beautiful. I could rarely embrace it.

Fear was my driving force, so almost immediately after a success, I had to keep pushing forward—getting better at school, sports, work, and life.

Success would come by the hand of God as a blessing, but in the fear-based pressure I created, it was never enough.

I was never good enough, even though, from God's perspective, I was already chosen, blessed, and validated without any acts of performance.

Instead of focusing on the blessings, I acted from a position of fear—fear of failure, fear of loss, fear of returning to a place of invisibility or worthlessness.

Every part of my walk in life became a performance, something I was being tested on.

Would I disappoint God?

Let down my mom?

Disappoint my coaches and family?

That fear drove my supposed "success." Ever heard the saying, "Fear of failure is one of the strongest motivators"?

That "success" comes at a cost, one I didn't realize until later in life.

Where else could fear be the motivating factor in life?

In a circle of friends?

In marriages?

In business deals?

In financial decisions?

In career choices?

I often fell into the trap of seeking approval from outside myself. In a sense, it was a deep protection method. My mind took the position that if I wasn't seen as perfect, I wouldn't survive. I'd be left on the curb, waiting until I metaphorically died again.

It was an extreme way to process things. My mind latched onto that idea after the pain of early childhood.

One thing I remember well is that I didn't feel much physical pain. I'd endure concussions, broken bones, and insane injuries while playing on the blacktop or in the streets of Philly.

As I write this, I'm just now connecting the dots—maybe my lack of physical pain was a way to be accepted.

If I put my body on the line, stretched into a defender or collided with a parked car to catch a pass, I would receive praise.

If I sacrificed my body, maybe people would accept me, maybe they would love me. In this hope of receiving love and acceptance, I developed a complete disregard for my own body.

It's miraculous that my body didn't completely give out on me. But just like in that heavenly space, the Lord held my body together in love, seeing the temple I couldn't see in my own body.

I was being accepted, and I could connect with friends on some level. I wasn't alone, so this must be working, I reasoned subconsciously.

A lack of sensation and connection to pain isn't necessarily a good thing, especially when it stems from an avoidance of perceiving pain out of fear.

My thoughts were coming from the language of the enemy, rooted in fear, rather than the language of God, rooted in love.

God progressively revealed to me the importance of questioning whether I was acting out of fear and scarcity or love and abundance.

It wasn't until my 40s that I could understand the clarity and freedom that question offers.

"Can I do everything someone asks of me in the classroom or on the court so that I'm accepted?"

This was the subconscious question I didn't realize I was asking with every people-pleasing, fear-based decision.

My teachers and coaches would praise me in grade school or high school, talking about my "talent," and unconsciously, I would return to that river and to God.

Or rather, I would return to the twisted version that my mind had latched onto.

It was subtle. I wasn't aware of where my mind was going. I felt pressure whenever praise or potential was directed my way.

How I received purpose, praise, potential, and words of affirmation—all of it felt like pressure, rooted in the moment the Lord spoke to me and everyone who followed.

I didn't even remember the heavenly experience anymore. The idea that I had to perform to meet everyone's expectations would slowly and steadily cripple me.

I couldn't see or feel it at the time. All I knew was that I was being accepted. I felt loved. It didn't matter what it was slowly costing me.

I would eventually "make it out" of Philly, as many of the older, tougher guys in the neighborhood would say to me.

It was as if I represented hope, the one who needed to escape the trap of inner-city life.

I didn't grow up getting beat up or running from the inner city because it was the worst place. In fact, I was protected by so many people—people I didn't even know.

It was the hand of God at work, not my own strength, which got me to where I wanted to be in life.

CHAPTER 9

MY OWN STRENGTH

I've been drawn to the warrior's way, the samurai code, and martial arts for as long as I can remember.

I believe God placed this on my heart, and in the sister books to this one, I believe you'll see the connection.

A warrior with his sword on his back. Old-school kung fu and samurai flicks, the warrior's way in 1980s and 1990s cartoons—all of these set the tone for my life.

All intentionally placed in my path.

This would come together in the form of certain types of anime, which depicted the life of a lone warrior. I related to the often challenging, even traumatic, childhoods of the main characters.

There was something about living with such honor, such power and self-command, such willpower that set the standard for all the comrades who fought alongside the mighty warrior.

I was drawn to this more than anything else in my older childhood, teenage, and young adult years.

I became less awkward, and although I still couldn't look at myself in the mirror with love, I could at least look.

I started to imagine myself walking with a sword on my back through the battlefield of life.

I was experiencing success and achievement. My older friends respected me, and I had a reputation for being tough in the area. I wouldn't back down and would give everything for the game, the win, the team.

I had a pretty intense stare at the time, often with headphones on, radiating a razor-sharp aura just like my favorite anime and warrior characters.

I accepted Jesus Christ as my Lord and Savior when I was 13 years old. My dad had beautifully created a life grounded in God and was working in ministry.

I still remember my favorite verse at the time, Philippians 4:13: All things are possible through Christ who strengthens me.

And perhaps, like other Christians, I took this to mean I could do all things. The words twisted in my head, trailing off so that Christ, the source of my strength, was forgotten.

Mix that verse with a warrior's spirit from the inner city, and my teenage years into young adulthood felt like a long series of battles that made up a war.

The soundtrack of my life matched what I listened to—a war soundtrack. The literal soundtracks of my favorite warrior movies, anime soundtracks, hardcore hip-hop, and classical music when I was on the razor's edge.

The next test in school that I needed to pass became the next battle I needed to win.

I had to "make it out" of the Philly streets. I had to succeed. I had to achieve.

If I had a big game or a track meet, the warrior's soundtrack played in my head, and unknowingly, I'd try to channel that energy.

Someone who had been in the presence of the Lord fell into that trap.

I would bring so much shame for doing this later in life, as if I were failing an all-knowing, all-loving God.

I'd slowly and steadily draw further away from Him and all the blessings in my life. Retreating into the delusion of my own strength.

If I succeeded, it was because I put in the work and deserved it.

If I failed, it was because I didn't want it enough. Didn't work hard enough. Didn't get mentally prepared for the test, the event, the exam—whatever held a performance component that I either won or lost.

Even if it was a team event, I always internally fought with myself. Why couldn't I have scored 60 points or won every event?

I let pressure mount everywhere. If things weren't going well with my family back home when I left for college, I believed it was because I wasn't there.

One of my failures in my last high school meet was a passcode I used for the first few years of college. I would never forget how I let my team down, even though we won the event.

From the outside, it looked like I had everything under control, like I was well put together.

The desire to make my mom proud and never give her anything more to worry about added another layer of intensity. Fueling my walk through the battlefield.

My awareness of my connection to God shifted further and further away. I relied more and more on my own strength.

As if life is a test, and God sits on the throne like a human king, testing who is worthy.

This is the same God who came to earth and died for our sins, who washed our feet, who served us.

It would take decades for me to cleanse this distorted view of a human king as God, even though I was blessed to stand right in front of Him!

During that time in my life, success came only by the grace of God, though I believed it was all due to my own strength.

I robbed God of His due glory, yet He still fed me, held me, and lifted me up.

I continued to choose to get stronger in my own strength.

To achieve, to gain glory, to excel.

My first year and a half in college was the first time I ran away from the pressure that gripped my neck.

I cared little about class. I was outside of the pressure to perform at home, and it felt like freedom. In reality, I was just running away—unable to discern what God was calling me to and what I was doing out of pressure.

I faded into the background until the end of my second year when a change in my family occurred.

My mom was diagnosed with a neurological condition. I was floating around, unsure of what I wanted to do with my life. I needed motivation.

My mom sacrificed her life for her children. The only way I could think of to repay her was by dedicating my career to her.

I decided to pursue physical therapy and dedicate my career to my mom. My graduate school, my patients, and many others have heard that part of my story.

What I didn't share was the immense amount of work I thought I needed to put in to reach that goal.

For those three years, and for the rest of my early adulthood and career, my soundtrack was the intense battle scenes from my favorite anime. Back against the wall, the warrior would succeed.

Sword on my back, every test, every standardized exam, every graduate admission process became the enemies that stood in my way.

A good friend of mine once asked if I was unconsciously seeking these challenges.

I was unknowingly seeking challenges just like the main character on a battlefield. I needed another victory to prove myself.

It wasn't until recently, after doing deep work on myself, that I realized this was a way of validating my existence. Seeking external validation that I could hold onto, proving my worth to be loved.

My desire to appear perfect, to always have the answer, to always succeed despite the circumstances. This pushed and pulled me to places that were not part of God's intent for me.

He exists in infinity, past and future. He is not surprised by it.

Every breath is a blessing from God, and so were each of those victories. Without the Lord, none of them would have existed. These are lessons I have only recently learned.

Even in my relationship and eventual first marriage—without a doubt, God's miraculous hand brought us together.

Yet, I idolized my own strength. I believed I could make it succeed.

Even though both our parents were divorced, I thought that with my strength, we could ensure that would never happen to us.

I'm better than the statistics. We're better than our parents. Give me a challenge, and I'll succeed!

Blessings upon blessings, success in my career—they all came pouring in. All I saw were victories and achievements.

I became more arrogant, believing these were the results of my hard work, good behavior, or something I "deserved."

I began to twist the idea that I had to keep all female friends at a distance. I thought I would be putting myself at risk of being unfaithful to my wife.

Performance and pressure again. How could I succeed where others had failed in marriage?

Frantic and full of fear, pride, and arrogance—these were not the thoughts of God.

Flawed thinking and a lack of trust in myself and in God to bring the people into my life that I needed.

I cut female friends out of my life, kept them at arm's length—all to appear perfect, hoping I could control the outcome and succeed in marriage.

The only woman I should have a loving friendship with is my wife—that was the lie my mind painted as truth, convincing me that I needed to be perfect in order to be loved.

The lines of having "too good a friendship" with another woman became blurred.

I felt shame when a friend reached out to me for help in her recovery, but I had deleted her contact information.

Only by the miraculous hand of God was I able to figure out who it was—a decision that left me feeling such deep shame.

With no priorities, I swung to the opposite extreme immediately afterward, vowing, "I will never let a friend of the opposite gender feel like I abandoned them again."

I felt I had failed as a friend just because I didn't want to be viewed as too close to another woman.

This had nothing to do with anyone else and everything to do with my attempt to appear perfect, to please literally everyone.

In doing so, I lost sight of the priorities God had gifted me in my family because I had no priorities.

My mind was scattered, taking on everything.

I was starting to unravel.

I had twisted the view of being perfect into something God had never called me to. Even in my flawed, erratic thinking, He was there, though I thought I could handle it all on my own.

"I'm as good as my results," was my mantra. My worth steadily became defined by what I could do for others.

I was gifted with three beautiful children. I didn't cherish them the way that boy in the river, whose last dying wish was to be a father, would have.

Even in my career, my inspiration for pursuing neurological physical therapy became a foothold for my overconfidence, idolization of outcomes, and complete forgetfulness of God in all that I did.

I trusted only my ability to research, find answers, diagnose, and successfully treat a rare neuro-vestibular disorder.

To create a program, to be one of the first to find a connection in this condition.

To be perfect—all out of fear of not being loved, out of pride in my own strength, and arrogance to believe I had achieved these things on my own.

I worked insane hours, chasing goals and business strategies, taking on more and more. "Give me your load," I'd say in my actions.

I carried everything—my patients, my business, my career, my family—taking it all on without any understanding of God-given priorities. I kept letting everything pile on.

There were times when I went six months sleeping just one hour a night, working nearly twenty-hour days, all in an effort to succeed through my own strength.

"I just need to work harder, go further, push beyond, and get to the next level," I told myself.

I'm a warrior who doesn't quit until success comes. I let that image define me.

"If you don't have it, you just didn't work hard enough or want it enough." I let that falsehood become truth in my mind.

I distinctly remember when I prayed, "God, I got this. I'm good— I'm going to do this my way."

I didn't have it, and I don't got this without Him. A realization that would come over a decade later.

The hand of God dipped into a river and gave me life again. Like Jonah with God, like Elijah in the cave, He fed me, nourished me, and blessed me.

How could I have the audacity to deny Him? (Another shame I would have to cleanse later in life.)

Before I could wash away that shame, I would have to face the breaking point of my strength.

CHAPTER 10

DEATH OVER DISHONOR

One of the things I loved most about the samurai in movies, documentaries, or shows was their honor. They lived by bushido, the code of the warrior, and often lived and died with honor as depicted in those stories.

The idea of "death over dishonor" resonated deeply with me. I can't count how many times I told myself, "I would die before..." It wasn't something I said lightly.

I would die before I wouldn't live with my children, and I would die before I would get a divorce or leave my wife.

Given my last breath, this twisted, self-centered view of these gifts might make sense.

And yet, here I am—a man who once said those things, now divorced and living apart from his children.

The idea of not kissing my children on their foreheads each night was openly my worst nightmare.

Living apart from them meant, in my mind, that I had failed as a father, a husband, and a man.

That was not allowed. I would not allow it. I would rather die than let that happen.

I worked excessive hours. There were times when I would forget who my kids' teachers were or what grade they were in.

I was so disconnected, yet I was physically present.

I was still succeeding, or so I thought—I just needed to keep going, to break through.

Maybe this is what God meant by "changing the world." I was doing it "on my own," yet His words were still there, even more twisted by my own strength.

I studied every business book, leadership book, podcast, and guru I could find, placing my hopes in someone who had achieved what I thought God was calling me to do.

"Comparison kills contentment"—another beautiful word from God through a sermon. I chose to keep looking to others for guidance on how to mystically reach the place where God wanted me.

As if I were turning in my test to God, showing Him what I had done in my own strength.

When all He wanted was to walk hand in hand with me, to do life together.

My back was against the wall, just where I subconsciously liked it.

"I do my best work here," I told myself. "I just need my sword, and I'll defeat all the enemies holding me back from the life I want."

I didn't even know what life I was pursuing. I was hectically pushing, taking on more load, thinking, "I can still do this. I can take more. I would rather die than give up."

I made so many life changes during this period, all in search of purpose.

"I would rather die than give up on my family and my children," I told myself. Despite how absent I was, they lovingly supported me.

They were there when I came home, and the most precious gift—to kiss them goodnight—was something I preserved each night, even if I didn't connect with them at any other time.

My worst nightmare was living apart from my children. "I won't be like my dad," I thought.

I would be there, at least physically, even if I wasn't there mentally or emotionally.

I was more connected to my children when I was serving overseas than during this time of my life.

Still, they loved their daddy, knowing how much I was working. They could see that my job seemed more important to me, even though they were my true priority.

"I'll die before I'm not with my children. I can't survive without them."

As far as I can remember, I've had an issue with how Simon Peter is often portrayed in the church. People joke about him, saying they would never deny God or criticizing him as a poor disciple.

According to biblical records, Simon Peter is still the only human being to walk on water.

I believe this is intentional. If he, among Jesus' disciples, could deny the Lord, who among us could confidently say, "I would never deny the Lord"?

In a sense, that's exactly what I was saying in that moment—that I had complete control over every variable in my life, every circumstance, and all outside forces.

Who but God can say that?

I'm still working through this with God. I believe this is where His guidance on not making promises or taking vows comes from.

It's not that the Lord will intentionally test you, but what about God's grace?

I continued to walk right into the illusion that I controlled everything in my life.

"I'll die before I leave my wife and children."

What happens when the choice between death and the thing someone says will never happen, happens?

Whether or not those were the only two choices, my mind reached a twisted place. It felt like the only options were to not live, or to live on in what I saw as shame and failure.

More simply, I asked myself: Is it more honorable to die or to live in the shame I believed awaited me?

The shame that would take years to realize was never mine to bear and may be the furthest thing from the God of all Heaven and Earth.

The answer I found in my own strength, apart from God, was just the warrior's code in those moments.

I saw things in black and white, missing the gray areas of the situation.

Missing the infinite color spectrum, not just the gray. I realize that now.

Maybe you or someone you love knows what it feels like to see only two options.

By His grace, God had a different answer.

If I ever slip into that space again, or if you do, He will have a different answer in love, joyfully rushing in.

I chose to live, not knowing what it would look like, fearing the shame that awaited me. His presence was there.

CHAPTER 11

THE FLOOR

I've reached my breaking point twice in my life, moments when I thought I couldn't take any more.

The first was when my business venture fell through. I wasn't sure how I could feed my family—I had given everything I had.

I had worked tirelessly, marketed, networked, and scratched and clawed to make the opportunity work.

It still failed. I had given everything I could in my own strength, even though I had told God, "I've got this."

Still, I asked, "Where were you, Lord? You let this happen to us."

All I could see was everything falling apart, so sleep-deprived I didn't know which way was up or down.

I lay on the floor in my bedroom, curled into a ball, crying. The kind of sobbing where each breath feels like it might be your last.

It felt like I was drowning in the river again. I had tried everything I could think of to save not just myself, but my family.

I used every strategy, every technique. I was desperate and lay there unfulfilled, facing an uncertain future, not wanting to take another breath.

As I lay on the floor in my desperation and despair, I could see and feel the Lord running to me.

It felt as tangible as the river, so much so that I pushed Him away as He attempted to wrap His arms around me.

For years, I let the enemy twist that experience into shame.

"Who would push away the Lord?" the enemy would whisper, as I let shame color the experience of the Lord rushing to my side to be with me.

Years later, I realized that He was already back with me immediately, holding me as I lay on the floor sobbing.

I think of *The Chosen* where they depict the scene of Peter walking on water and the Lord holding him. That's what it was like.

We have a God who loves us so unconditionally that we can feel it in some of our human relationships, and the vertical connection to God is on another level of love.

The second time I met the floor was right after my separation when my kids and ex-wife moved away.

The Lord knew I needed someone there, and by His grace, our dog was with me. Our dog's lick at that moment on the floor was such a precious gift.

This was my worst nightmare. I had made the choice to live and not remain in my marriage, which meant I had chosen not to live with my kids every day.

They needed to be with their mother. I knew what divorce looked like from my own experience, and I accepted that expectation.

No matter what, I would no longer be physically with my children every day. No matter what.

Laying on the floor, drowning again, curled up just like I was in the river, being flipped and tossed every which way.

All my efforts to stabilize my family had failed.

The choices I made to use my voice—which I didn't even really know from a lifetime of people-pleasing—and the inauthenticity of doing that for most of my marriage had caused so much hurt.

The pain I caused my ex-wife by choosing not to trust myself, my voice, and her—all of it from "trying in my own strength."

I reached the limit of what I could do to hold a marriage with children together.

I had failed as a husband, and my worst nightmare of being away from my children came true. I faced certain failure as a father, curled up on the floor.

The Lord opened another space, almost becoming tangible again, just like in the river.

This time, He took me back to that moment after I had accepted death and heard His word about changing the world.

Lovingly, He gave me guidance that I still walk in today and pray I will walk in for all the days of my life.

The greatest commandment.

To love the Lord my God with all I am. To love my neighbor as (and) myself.

I still have a lifetime to learn about love as God sees it. It was simple—not easy.

To simply love—that is how I get to change the world.

If you're like me, loving yourself—the last part of that commandment—is the most difficult.

Tears and sobbing, lost on the floor again, drowning again, He gifted me with a reminder of being in that heavenly place. Clarity on what changing the world would mean for my walk.

We have access to an all-loving God who wants us to seek Him, who lovingly gives us clarity. We get to lean on Him every step of our lives.

He is not a distant ruler, nor a religious elite sitting inaccessible on His throne.

He came down and was born in a manger.

He walks among His children, rushes to us, and is right there when we sink, holding us.

He kneels next to us and loves us at our level. He is a king and ruler unlike anything experienced in the world.

Please hear me—I did experience depression and anxiety, and I needed professional help to walk into the more that God had for me.

I would invite you to open your mind to see where God might be working and through sources that may not seem like they're from God.

I got up off the floor. My pup, ready to lick my tears, stood by as I faced what I thought was shame waiting for me.

I decided to take the next best step forward. I had done everything in my own strength—my children were apart from me, and my marriage had failed.

I prayed and committed to walking with the Lord every step from then on because this life going forward wouldn't look like what I expected anymore.

That's where my miraculous happens—beyond what I expected, walking hand in hand with God.

I had expected death as a boy and then as a man. Instead, God gave me so much more.

CHAPTER 12

THE RIVER

Over the next couple of years, I would learn to trust the Lord and His word.

He set my priorities for me. Rooted in the greatest commandment. It was actually quite freeing. For the first time, I had clear, definitive priorities.

He was teaching me how to love unconditionally, as He sees it—starting with my children.

With God as my priority and center, I had access to infinite love, not just the finite love I could generate on my own.

It was beautiful to see how love opened new possibilities to connect, and how much trust I had to have to live apart from my children.

It didn't feel beautiful in the moment—this was my "worst nightmare," after all. Gradually, I could see the beauty God was working right from where I was.

I needed reassurance. The Lord gave it to me in the first promise I felt He placed over me since living apart from my children.

Through a word during a sermon, He spoke to me, saying He had my children in His care. In that moment, I felt peace.

They were in His hands. I realized that no matter how many times I Face Timed them each day, I had to trust that they were safe in His arms and that He was providing for them and my former spouse.

He guided me to do everything within my power to continue providing for them, even from a distance.

Day to day, I was just trying to make sure I had enough to fly out and see my kids every other weekend, ensuring they felt loved even though I was stationed in a different state.

My own childhood experience guided me—I didn't want them to ever think their dad didn't love them.

So, all the extra money I had, I put toward flights to see them, as God put it on my heart.

I was no longer married, not dating or in a relationship—and laughably, I couldn't even afford to eat out by myself.

I felt like I deserved this, penance for ending my marriage and getting divorced.

A punishment, especially after telling my family about the divorce, I felt I deserved even more. Residual pain from my own family growing up and our dad.

I felt lonely, and I was so focused on seeing and talking with my kids that it felt like all I could do at the time.

Yet, He spoke a promise over me—that I would be blessed with a miraculous relationship and marriage with a woman.

Through words in various sermons or prayers, He even started to describe her qualities.

Just as is my experience with the Lord, it wasn't about what the world said I deserved or even what I felt I deserved.

I thought, "This is where I'll stay, Lord. I'll sacrifice my life until the kids get to college, and then maybe I'll consider dating again."

A Lord who sacrificed Himself for our sins—and here I was, thinking some altruistic sacrifice of my own would please Him.

I can't count how many times I've tried to climb onto a cross that is already empty, all in an attempt to please someone.

When friends would ask about my dating life, I felt too awkward, too much of a loser to date. I was so disconnected from the idea of courting a potential mate that it seemed like it would take a miracle.

God still wanted more for me. I believe He wants more for all of us.

One thing I frequently hear from God is that when we don't get what we want, it's never because we asked too much of Him.

It's because we didn't ask enough. If you believe, as I do, that God is for us and wants to give us good things—that He is not "stealing" from us or "teaching us a lesson" with a ruler in His hand, ready to punish us at every turn—then you can be free to experience the loving Creator He is.

The lesson of holding on too tightly to expectations—when God wants to exceed those expectations—is something I continuously get to learn and experience.

Everything will look like a disappointment when you believe God is not for you.

Eventually, I started dating again, even being open to online and app dating, which I had been against all my life.

Nothing that God had promised had come yet, and I needed to stay open and be joyful.

This wasn't a task I needed to complete. Another checklist to get to my goals. He reminded me of that frequently.

I got to enjoy the process of meeting new people and being open to what this promised woman would look like.

I had thoughts and expectations of who this person was, where she lived, what she looked like—and God washed over me with qualities from women in the Bible, a combination so unbelievable that I asked God if this person was even possible.

God had already set the standard for the miraculous by bringing my first wife into my life. He would not disappoint. Even when I wanted to lower my standards, He never did.

I joke that God needs to make Himself visible to me and speak out loud because I'm so hard-headed and logical—that's how He reaches me.

So, by His grace, I started paying attention when the miraculous began to happen.

I had the most beautiful first date, with so many "coincidences" that only God could be at work. All the miraculous movements He orchestrated to get us to that first date.

I was in a walking boot after surgery while I was overseas, and she had hurt her foot (which we later found out was broken). Both of us had injuries to our left foot.

So, amidst the joy of getting to know each other, we were both limping around after our coffee shop date.

Where did we limp next? Down by the river, of course—a beautiful scene filled with life and joy. Life energy fed by our connection.

I had been by rivers, oceans, seas, and lakes without any fear of bodies of water since my drowning. I had learned to swim immediately, as my mom recommended.

There are a few places where the water rushes on this river, including a spot where people cross along rocks to the other side.

I realized, as I walked across rocks in the middle of rushing water, that I had no abnormal fear of falling in. That, in itself, is miraculous.

The beautiful river where we would walk from then on.

Nature, energy, connection, love—all the beautiful things converging along this river.

Bringing beauty, joy, love, and purpose.

The flowing river, just like that heavenly light, feeding the trees, plants, greenery, the birds, the fish—everything.

I look forward to writing our book together, which will elaborate more on this time walking together along the river.

The insights God gives us. The talks we have. The love that surrounds us and fills us, flowing freely through us by His grace to those who need it.

This river, God used to weave a beautiful connection in love that I like to think He saw when He placed me back on earth. He saw her on the other side of my drowning, unable to cry tears of my own as I accepted death.

He saw my children, whom I thought I'd never have as water filled my body. They were already formed in His eyes as the beautiful gifts He gave me in love.

He saw the miraculous connection with my father. I shared this experience with him for the first time, in preparation for this book and to honor him.

He saw the miraculous connection with my father. As I shared this experience with him for the first time, in preparation for this book and to honor him.

My dad and I, of course, had the most beautiful conversation, reliving the time around the river in our lives, in the ocean.

As if the very water itself was cleansing all that didn't belong to either of us.

The fear of my dad being disappointed in me, the fear that he would be hurt that I am writing this book—all washed away by our Father who knows no ends.

My dad, who had his own experience with fear of the water, stood with me in the water. We cut through the niceties and connected honestly with our experiences. Only the God who does miracles every day could make that happen.

The Lord saw the miraculous— so much I've already seen—and here's to the more He has for me, my love, our children, and all our loved ones who surround us.

Next, I get to continue to wipe off anything that doesn't belong to me and walk in the miraculous He has for us!

CHAPTER 13

RELEASE

Even after I met my love, I still held onto the pressure of "changing the world."

I knew it wasn't in my own strength anymore and that I simply needed to love the Lord, myself, and others.

And yet, I didn't know what the next step was.

I had talked about the drowning experience with various close people in my life and family. However, I always stopped before the part where I accepted death and stood before the Lord.

That was until my second date with my love. I had asked for the miraculous. The Lord didn't hold back, even though I wanted to.

He prompted me to share, and I kept sharing. I bargained with God, saying I would only speak more if she asked, she kept digging.

I ended up sharing with her something I had never shared in depth with anyone before—my experience with God and what He spoke to me.

It could've easily flowed that way with anyone else who started down that path. It never did until that day.

She said in that moment she wasn't going to be the last to hear this.

Despite my thinking, "You sure will be." Here we are.

The Lord was at work, beginning to release many things that were holding me back from walking into the more He had for me.

I had described His words as pressure, something that is not in the character of God.

So together, we visualized, deeply meditated, and moved back into that space.

God guided the woman who was called to walk with me through this experience, helping me reclaim it for the Lord.

He took me back into that heavenly space during a loving worship service where we were in worship for hours that felt like days or weeks of joy in Heaven.

All of this reclaimed the experience—the loving hands of the Lord wrapped around me.

The light and His essence. An entire dimension hugging me—if you could imagine something like that.

It flowed so seamlessly with His word from when I was on the floor: to walk simply in His love.

The power I get to lean on going forward is love—His love, which gave all of existence. It breathed life into our lungs.

At the center of all things heavenly and earthly, I get to steward this love—the most powerful force in the universe, a force so strong that evil cannot even stand in its presence.

That power.

It's so beautiful how, in Him, we can reclaim what the enemy tries to separate us from.

Our relationship with a loving God and our connection to each other.

I had, and still have, more releasing to do.

My next transformative experience would come at the beginning of an incredible immersive leadership experience.

The details seemed simple, but a word from God came straight through the lead instructor.

She shared an experience that was actually from her husband, and it helped open my mind to this experience and every experience to follow that week—a significant week for growing into God's purpose.

He had pulled everything together to make this course happen. I knew God wanted me there.

My expectations were high, and as is His nature, He exceeded them.

By His grace and through our instructor flowing in the voice of the Lord, I stepped up for the activity.

She was given exactly what I needed in that moment, as if the Lord had allowed her to peer into my soul.

She spoke out, reading my deep emotions that I'd been so good at hiding, as if she were reading the pages of a book. Only our Lord could create something so clear in that moment.

Trust.

Would I be able to trust?

What is trust?

Do I trust myself?

Do I trust anyone else?

Do I trust God?

I could quickly answer yes, but then I would want to control the road and what it looked like. That's not trust.

"Go to the place I'll show you"—that's His language, and it's difficult to follow. Ask Abraham, the father of faith.

I was feeling pretty good about trusting the vertical portion of the cross—my relationship with God.

The horizontal portion of the cross is another story. The second part of the greatest commandment: Love others as yourself.

Love my neighbor as myself. You could easily substitute trust for love.

"Wait a minute, Lord, you said love them, not trust them."

Whoa! Revelation in that moment: Can I say I love my neighbor if I don't trust them?

Only you can answer that question for yourself, and with God.

My answer, as God calls me to walk in the love He has for us, is no— I can't truly love my neighbor or myself if I don't trust either.

I come back to that word from God: Be as innocent as doves and as shrewd as serpents. I don't get to be naïve out of ignorance.

I do get to walk in the ultimate power of His love—kindness.

In kindness, I get to extend my trust to others. That was the prevailing word of my entire experience, starting at that moment and building to heights I had never experienced.

I received our instructor's blessing, and she led with her authentic self during the exercise, giving me exactly what I needed to experience.

Joy and peace in being open and vulnerable. I realized I could be vulnerable and not die.

I could be vulnerable and still be loved. Not by everyone, and that's okay.

I could relax my protection against hurt, against self-hate.

Since I started reconnecting with God, He has been teaching me how to love myself.

I had to revisit Chapter 13, where I talked about whom God wanted me to learn to love unconditionally first.

Unconsciously, I said my children. Their response after the divorce was my focus.

He was actually teaching me how to love myself unconditionally first.

Even writing this book, I need His help. He reminds me every day where my intentions and gratitude need to start.

For me, my love, my children, and all those around us to walk into abundance, I need to love and care for myself unconditionally.

Letting that flow of love run freely, without any blockages or clogged pipes—filling me up, then all those around me.

In that moment, I waited, as the hand of God worked through our instructor's hand to free me from a huge block, allowing me to walk into everything He has for me.

His words of open vulnerability and trust, coupled with wisdom, continues to guide me to this day. I need that reminder each day.

Thankfully, we have a God who is excited to give us a hand, another reminder, another whisper to show us the way.

He's not the frustrated authority figure we might imagine.

He enjoys giving us everything we need.

When you think of the Garden of Eden before the fall, did we not have everything we needed in Him? Is that not Heaven?

He knows we need Him to walk this out. He knows what we're up against in this world.

I learned to see God as for me, and that He uses all things for my good if I'm open to seeing it. I hope for many others to see this too.

I've been so blessed to experience others who see God as I felt Him in His glory. He has lovingly connected them to my path, and I love sharing, during my prayers, the love I experience with God.

The joyful Father who loves His sons and daughters and all of life He created on earth. He is your biggest cheerleader, the one you don't see, dancing with joy when you receive a gift from Him.

That check you weren't expecting.

The miracle out of nowhere.

My experience of Him is not of a king out of touch with His servants.

He is a loving Father, Abba, Daddy, Papa, ruler of the universe, Christ the King—all of those things. I AM/Yahweh—insert whatever you need.

CHAPTER 14

───────

SIT AT YOUR FEET

I remember the first time I sat in my dad's classroom. I was about 12 or 13 years old. We were growing close again, splitting time between my mom and stepdad, and my dad and stepmom.

This was the first time I saw him teaching. I was sitting in his adult Sunday school class, or maybe it was a Wednesday night Bible study. It was the first time I had seen my dad as a teacher.

My dad had become more present in our lives, walking in new connection and salvation in Jesus. It was beautiful to see him walking in life with purpose.

A classroom full of students, all eager to learn, sat on the edge of their seats before the class even began. I, like many kids that age, had a seemingly disinterested look on my face as I waited for my dad to finish his class.

I held my father in high regard, but like many teens, I felt like I had better things to do. We could be watching a game, playing ball, or hanging out somewhere.

I could feel the excitement in the air—something special was about to happen.

I sat in my dad's classroom, the only non-adult there, fascinated by the lesson he taught on the Word.

He was engaging, challenging, and supportive. The joy in that classroom was palpable. More than that, the joy on my dad's face as he interacted with his students was beautiful.

I hung on to every word he taught and pondered it. I think I even took notes—not out of performance, but out of a genuine desire to soak up the teachings.

This was my father's gift from God, one of many, and the most prominent.

Not even my teenage tight lips could stay closed when I shared my thoughts with my dad on the way home.

"That was the best teaching experience I've had," I told him, "and it's a gift you should continue to pursue."

I'm still shocked at how easily that support flowed from my mouth.

Anyone in that class could see it. I think it meant a lot coming from a boy who didn't say much about things like that.

Maybe it was one of the first times God used me to give a word of encouragement to someone.

I would watch my dad finish his master's in theology, enter ministry, and then receive his doctorate in education, going on to have a long, successful career in education.

As a son, watching my dad continue to show up, even when it was hard, and keep pushing forward in life is inspiring. It's a testament to the man he is. He could have thrown in the towel at any time but didn't.

I remember one moment in particular that shaped how I saw my dad.

He had nominated my stepdad for a "Man of Character" award in the church for so lovingly raising my sisters and I.

I could feel the awkwardness in the lead pastor as he read it, and there could have been judgment and shame too.

"Someone else raising your kids" is not something that goes over well in the traditional church.

I saw my dad sit in it and stay in it in that moment.

I would hear him preach—more of a teacher than what most people called a preacher—sharing his own challenges growing up.

I am honored to have sat at his feet, learning from my dad.

Fast forward to a time in my life as a father.

I needed time to revisit what I sought during the two years when I just focused on flying to see my kids.

The Lord used that time to build a deep, loving connection with Him. I hope to continue to open up to and grow in as I live the rest of my life.

Those were my training grounds—many days and nights spent with just the Lord and me. Learning to hear His word and walk in it.

Feeling lonely, yet never alone—God was with me every single breath.

The great Teacher is always speaking, something I was challenged to realize since I actually heard His voice out loud early in life.

I had to learn that He spoke just as clearly during the two times I was on the floor in my lowest moments, and every single moment in between, if I was open to listen.

His guiding voice, a lamp lighting my feet to where we both want me to be.

What is a teacher, and where does his or her authority come from?

Jesus the Christ, our Lord and Savior. Our Rabbi/teacher/sensei?

The teachers of the law who had Jesus crucified?

My dad?

Me?

My children?

A beautiful visual I love is of the Lord of all the universe sitting at our feet, lovingly listening to our stories, our pains, our thoughts, as He walked the earth before His resurrection.

Yes, He taught with the ultimate authority, and He engaged with His students and disciples.

He also experienced life with us, sharing meals and wisdom. I love the picture of this loving Teacher.

I believe He still sits at the feet of His children, eager to hear their words, while feeding them the Word they need in that very moment.

Enter my love. My first experience seeing her speak at a church event while we were first dating. I had seen pictures and glimpses from previous events, but this one was live.

She delivered a powerful message. As she spoke, I could feel the Lord's presence—cheerfully with her, leaning in to hear her deliver a life-changing word.

The feeling of a cheering Father, so joyful and proud, so attentively listening and loving us in our moments: when we speak, give a talk on stage, teach our children, teach our neighbors, and engage with our loved ones.

It's like a spiritual high-five or fist bump, as the Lord who gives us our breath and our words, loves those moments for us.

I heard the term from our instructor at the leadership seminar: "sit at your feet."

An idea I often saw in dojos, martial arts, and movies of the same.

A sensei with their students eagerly waiting to hear their words. A Messiah who was God and taught.

He also sits at our feet, excited and proud as we rock the presentation, crush the event, and spread love during a performance.

That is my experience of the Lord—One from whom all knowledge comes.

Who also hears and listens to us, being with us in our moments as we speak, in a loving way like no other.

CHAPTER 15

CENTER

I've been wonderfully curious over the last few years about how Jesus stood during the time before His crucifixion.

What was His posture?

Standing in confidence—what did that look like for Jesus?

Maybe it's because I've been seeking confidence, or whatever that means, since I was a boy.

I was never satisfied with the common explanations of confidence. They never fit.

The Lord gave me a beautiful definition during a sermon at church. It started with faith. The pastor said, "Faith is confidence in God to..."

I diligently wrote down the rest of the statement, placing it in my notes.

At the time, I was navigating a new reality—living apart from my children and divorced.

I was also a precious son of God, loved more than I could imagine.

The Lord had me pause at "Faith is confidence in God."

My mathematical, logical mind almost immediately turned it into an equation.

I love how much the Lord understands me at a level no one else can.

Faith = Confidence (In God).

My confidence isn't in myself. I'm not a self-made man—far from it.

The miraculous happens arm in arm with the Lord, who parts the seas, dries up the Jordan, raises the dead (even now), and heals the sick and brokenhearted.

Faith is the confidence I had been seeking my whole life.

My confidence is rooted in the Creator of the universe, who wants to co-create with me.

He doesn't require me to pass 15 more tests to prove my worth. That is not the God of love who had a dove descend on Jesus and validate Him before He performed any public miracles.

I was so freed by the realization that my faith, or confidence, didn't hinge on me. It hinges on the One who never fails.

His yoke is light; my confidence is in Him. I get to give it to Him freely, allowing my pride to continue to die.

I felt like I was inching closer to standing with the confidence that the Lord stood in.

I still wanted to know—how did He stand in the presence of those who hated, persecuted, and killed Him?

What posture did the Lord take?

He placed it on my heart to seek more. I didn't simply accept, "It doesn't matter; He's God."

Then I had an experience with grounding and centering at the leadership training I mentioned earlier.

I had been in and out of martial arts training throughout my life.

This experience was different. This was the next step I was seeking in understanding how He stood.

An open body position—a vulnerable position—grounded and centered, starting with peace within my body and spirit.

This was the beginning of understanding how Jesus may have stood in His time before His death and resurrection.

Knowing He would be sacrificed, coming in as our most vulnerable form—a baby—the Creator of all Heaven and Earth.

The One who could have rained thunder at any time, as reminded by *The Chosen* when Jesus talks with James and John.

He lived in a position of ultimate vulnerability as God, and He was crucified for our sins.

Grounded and centered, connecting to the earth formed by God.

Tapping into the deepest places of love and starting from this position.

I'll let you experience this for yourself. As for me, the vision of the path to standing and walking like Jesus became clearer.

It helped that the Lord knew how much I love the martial arts language and spiritual groundedness. This was completely different than I had ever experienced—the hand of God around this exercise.

People can confuse this technique. Intimidation versus vulnerability.

In the presence of that heavenly space, with a power greater than all things, He lifted me up. He lovingly held me up so that I could stand in His presence.

I've often experienced the opposite. A person flaunts their presence or power to assert their position.

The enemy takes this stance—to flaunt power or position over someone.

I'm the first to admit I'd get pumped when I saw the main character power up in my favorite shows, ready to destroy legions of enemies.

The One who controls all and has all power has no need to prove He's powerful.

This is my experience of the Lord. It makes sense to me. Evil cowers before this power.

He chose to be vulnerable. He chose to surrender His life.

He could have called legions of angels. Turned His captors into pillars of salt. Flooded the world that very instant.

He maintained His powerful, vulnerable, open body position.

He loves dearly and cares for every child unconditionally. Using this power—the origin of all life—to serve, heal, bless, and love.

A concept foreign to much of this world.

I love how such a concept, often thought to be apart from God, could originate from Him. Connecting yoga, martial arts, dance, meditation, and the heavenly.

The ultimate form of grounding and centering in an open body position felt like I leaped to the next step in my "training."

The Lord graciously corrected me to consider the term "play" versus "training."

By God's grace, I gained a new technique!

I am able to stand confidently in Him.

Well not always—I'm still working on it. It feels like leaps and bounds toward walking in the miraculous.

Walking on water—or better yet, walking through the crowd.

CHAPTER 16

MOVE THROUGH THE CROWD

I remember so many times reading in the Gospels about how Jesus walked through the crowds.

He walked unmovable from His purpose by either the praise or the hate of those around Him.

Such a different concept.

The world often talks about ignoring the "haters" or walking without caring about what people think. Jesus cared and loved us deeply and kept walking. Unconditionally loved us and kept walking.

Jesus walked past the haters. He was also unmovable in His walk by the praise of others.

That's the most subtle and hardest thing to be aware of for me.

A popular character in one of my son's and my favorite shows, who was a boss and a real talent, said something profound.

The downside of being talented, gifted, and praised all the time is that it's very easy to become proud, arrogant, and disconnected.

I like praise so much more than hate. I like praise so much more than constructive feedback. I like praise so much more than a loving word from a loved one that I need to step into something God is calling me to.

Those are my defaults—what my human mind drifts to.

I had to reconcile and realize what latching onto praise does to me.

External validation, people-pleasing, seeds of arrogance.

Could I learn to accept positive and negative feedback without being judgment on my character?

I'm already loved, I'm already chosen to walk into everything God has for me.

It's also not about walking and not caring about anyone else.

He loved all of us so unconditionally that He gave His life, walking through the crowd deeply connected to what God called Him to do.

Grounded and centered, in a vulnerable open body position, I began to walk in this posture.

Then, just like one of my favorite songs says, I started seeing what God might see and walking like He might walk. A transcendent peace.

I've had fun in my book club with my son and going through illustrations of biblical stories.

One of the things I was most excited to see drawn was Jesus walking through the crowds when He was facing death. I remember reading about it so many times in the Bible or hearing the story in church.

It felt like it was glossed over every time. God highlighted it in my mind each time. It was like whenever someone preached on it, they just said, "He walked through the crowd," as if anyone could do that.

Facing certain death, the Lord walked through a crowd of people intent on killing Him. What?!

I saw an illustration with my son, it was so beautiful to share how awesome it was to see God in that way.

Then, *The Chosen* took it to the next level.

I already felt satisfied that the picture of Jesus walking through the crowd in His hometown, as they intended to kill Him, was done so well.

Then the team at *The Chosen* stepped it up another notch.

Facing certain death and the anger of His hometown, He didn't force everyone into submission, He didn't turn them to stone, He didn't snap them into nothing.

In unconditional, infinite love and power, He walked right through them!

I knew it—His word that I get to walk in life as He does. I could see an example of how it looks.

"How do I get to that, Lord?!" That was my response as I had to rewind what I just saw in that episode.

Enter my training at the leadership seminar: grounded, centered, open body position, vulnerable, no guards, no rage—just love and trust in the Lord and walk.

This was the start—or better yet, the next step. The Lord began to reveal how I could connect this to how He walked if I chose to: ultimate vulnerability, incomprehensible power, and unconditional love mixed into one.

This was like the baby step of what the Lord did in perfection. "Ok, I got it. So, I get to learn this, and I get to walk in this."

Boldness—another quality I pulled from those two illustrations of Jesus walking through the crowds.

A quality I've feared much of my life, as a people-pleaser. Boldness might hurt someone's feelings.

There is a lot of boldness required to walk in that position and with that groundedness—enough to walk up to those with murderous intent and walk right through them.

Loving them and caring for them, not intimidation. I couldn't imagine a better way to depict that balance.

I even got to experience a wonderful activity, putting walking into action—facing whether I trust myself, trust another person, trust my surroundings. To feel the energy of connectedness, love, and joy exchanged—magical.

The scenery in the seminar room was so beautiful. The beautiful souls I had the privilege to share a room with, the people I get to walk the earth with.

Wow, learning to come from a space of joy and love as God has been guiding me. Such a cherished moment.

To tap into His overflowing joy and love freely and walk vulnerably toward another human being—a beautiful feeling.

I'll leave your experience to be yours, should you choose to experience something like that.

It's so beautiful. A word the Lord likes to remind me of is the one He gave His disciples: to go out as innocent as doves and shrewd as serpents.

We get to be vulnerable and also wise. I'm learning the balance— open body position, vulnerable, yet not walking off the edge of a cliff and calling it vulnerability.

I'm not sure of the depth of what God will have me walk into as He walked into.

Careful that in my self-sacrificing tendencies I don't try to take Jesus' place on the cross when He's already resurrected.

He died as a sinner so that we could live as if we hadn't—another beautiful word from God through a sermon.

I believe He calls me, and all of His children, to walk on water.

To walk in the miraculous. This feels like He is joyfully walking, about to start into a run with me on the water.

Just like another beautifully artistic rendition of Jesus with us in the movie *The Shack*.

CHAPTER 17

THE CLIMB

It wouldn't be long before our Lord would call me to put this into practice even more.

I believe the Lord touched my experience at the leadership seminar—years of growth packed into a week.

I wasn't sure what was next. I felt God was just getting warmed up, excited to see me walking into more of the new me.

The version of myself I had pictured every now and then over the past year.

Cloaked in white light, surrounded by and flowing with love, power, and confidence—faith.

Becoming more like the image we are all intended to be, like our Maker and nothing less.

Not through effort, but through the joy of being our uniquely formed selves, the best version of who we are.

After all, our Maker is Yahweh—the great "I AM." Insert the best qualities of yourself.

I faced an obstacle, and in learning my initial lesson about trust, I held my overly analytical tendencies at bay. This was one I had to walk in faith.

The word I needed would be given to me at just the right moment.

"Trust me," I heard from the Lord.

Facing this obstacle, my thoughts were:

Could I do this in my own strength?

Probably.

"But do you want to?" I felt God ask.

"No, I get to trust the people supporting me." That horizontal part of the cross.

I get to trust others, not just Him and not just myself.

I chose to walk in that trust—one step, then the next.

Then the word came from the Lord in that moment:

Trust, trust, trust, trust, trust, trust...

Every step, trust them.

Next step, trust them.

Could I step in my own power? Of course.

But that is beneath what I'm called to.

The miraculous is what He calls all of us to—I believe this.

Another moment I looked forward to, depicted in *The Chosen*, was Jesus and Simon walking on the water.

Walking on water, the space of walking in the miraculous every day, is something I believe He wants for us.

One step, focused on Him, trusting Him—and for me during this activity, trusting my brothers and sisters in this world.

Trust, trust, trust, trust, trust... then a huge step in trust, and I was there.

To the outside, maybe it seemed like I got there in my own strength.

The comments after the event support that.

In that moment, it was the closest I've come to walking on water, walking on air.

I felt like I could fly, seeing a path to walk in the miraculous.

I don't plan on stepping onto air anytime soon, but I also loved the end of the movie *The Shack*, when the main character prepares to step onto the water as he did when he was with Jesus.

I don't know exactly what's in store for me on this earth, but I also need God to remind me at each step what I need to live abundantly.

Each step to walk in the miraculous with Him.

Apart from Him, we are nothing. He gladly gives us the words, the tools, the reassurance.

Another twist of the enemy, which was revealed in that event was the idea that I had to do life alone, get to the top alone.

The notion of a "self-made man" or success by my own strength has to die every day in my life.

I choose and commit, by His grace, to continuously let that die— the idea that I have to do this alone to prove something.

I flew through that event, apparently looking like I wasn't trying, from the outside looking in.

I want to tap into that every day. I pray that when I need reminding, I'm open to hearing the voice of the Lord quickly... trust, trust, trust, and fly!

I believe this is the path to abundance that He has placed me on— miraculous abundance.

I believe He wants that for all of us. Heaven.

We can experience pieces of this on earth— in the miraculous gifts He has for us.

CHAPTER 18

MIRACULOUS TOGETHER

I faced another challenge in my leadership training. This time, it had to be done with a partner.

By God's beautiful design, I had already done it on my own earlier in my life.

God let me sit in that moment and consider how I wanted to approach this event.

Would I bark orders because I had already proven myself on my own?

Would I complete the task whether or not my partner finished, thinking, "As long as one of us finishes, we complete the task, right?"

I reflected on all the relationships in which I had gone ahead in my own strength—marriage, business, life.

All those previous thoughts and logical mechanisms died further in me that day. I pray they stay dead for the rest of my life.

I committed to doing this *with* my partner, together. All those performance-oriented thoughts swirling in were like the waves as Peter walked on the water.

Would I choose to stay focused on the Lord and my partner and *be* a loving partner, rather than just *do* the event?

The Lord had me sit right in the middle of seeing every relationship—past and future.

Trust, trust, trust... even if I think I know the answer.

Who I am in the process and the qualities I display are light-years above the logistics, as high as heaven is above earth.

I saw my dearest loved ones in those moments. I realized I don't want to do this life without them, every step, ever again.

I get to walk in everything God has for me and my loved ones.

I get to be a loving, committed partner with them.

Whether it's my significant other/wife.

Whether it's my children. (It's interesting—God wants to partner with us, His children. I just saw that connection as I wrote this.)

Whether it's my dad.

Whether it's my mom.

Whether it's a friend, a colleague, or a new business partner.

Trust, trust, trust, trust, trust—and love.

The result of that loving support, building on each other, was a beautiful sight to be part of and, from others watching, a sight to behold.

My experience of God is that He wants the miraculous, the transcendent, the magnificently beautiful for us.

That will look different for each person and their relationship with God—their purpose and what they are willing to receive.

My love and I practice visualizations, meditations, and the like to further tune into God's voice.

He uses all things for our good, and I remember hearing a word from God: "We are the ones we are waiting for."

In the talk, it was primarily to promote personal investment in our day-to-day actions.

I feel the Lord saying He wants to use us.

Which is really no different than hearing "change the world" from Him. That actually sounds just like the God of my experience.

That we all have a part in all this. He wants to partner with us, co-create with us.

The spiritual high-fiving, fist-bumping God after a big event—that's my experience of a God so full of joy and love and power that evil has no choice but to move away.

He's our ultimate partner in all this, with us every single step. The loving, all-powerful Creator of the universe partners with us each day to be miraculous together.

As we partner with each other in trust and love, we step into the miraculous together—not trying to achieve an objective, but to walk in abundance.

CHAPTER 19

THE GIFT

When I was on the floor the second time, God gave me a revelation about how to change the world—simply by loving Him, others, and myself, as commanded in the greatest commandment.

Lying in my worst nightmare, apart from my children, He gave me a second revelation: He had fulfilled my two regrets from my last breath.

I wished for two things: someone to love me just as I am (in my mind, a wife) and children to share my life with.

That was it—nothing more, nothing less.

In that moment, He freed me to see that He was the one who loved me unconditionally, no matter what, knowing everything about me—greater than I could ever be loved by anyone who walked this earth.

That was a liberating moment. It took me until the last chapter of my book to remember it—or rather, for God to prompt me exactly where to place it.

No woman would ever have to try to fill that role again. I would never have that regret because God had fulfilled it. And He had already blessed me with children.

The Lord, whom I love so dearly, knew what I meant.

With a big smile on my face, He knew I meant a wife, so only as He could, He cleansed the regret, preventing any other woman from feeling the kind of pressure she should never feel walking into my life.

Standing where only God can stand in our lives, not even our spouses or dearest loved ones can stand.

So, I would be in a position to receive this glorious gift—another chance to be married.

Someone who doesn't have to fill God's shoes and who, in God's likeness, can love me just as I am.

How could anyone love me just as I am if I don't use my voice, if I people-please to hide my truest desires?

How could anyone love me just as I am if I simply don't love myself?

These are commitments, wrapped in His grace, that I get to walk out every day.

A gift, wrapped in a gift, given in a gift—the layers in which the Lord works are astounding.

As high as heaven is above earth, so are His ways above ours.

I pray, by His grace and in my commitment, that I continue to walk in the precious gift of this love.

I used to wonder—did I actually make it out of that river?

Am I on life support somewhere?

Is this the Lord giving me one last, really long, life-like dream to experience all of this?

Every moment is a gift.

Every chance to use my voice is a promise fulfilled.

My voice matters, and so does yours.

By all rights and logic, what I deserved drowning in that river was a watery grave.

What should have been my end—never finding love, never fathering children, never going on a date, never driving a car legally, never meeting all of the wonderful, beautiful people who have become the tapestry of my life.

The Lord loves you all so much, it's hard to imagine His love.

In that moment of my last breath, I thought it just wasn't meant for me.

The Lord, by His grace and love, scooped me out and said, "Yes, it is, son."

Without an ounce of pity in His light or eyes, He gave me purpose, wrapped in the gift of another day on this earth.

Is that not like every day?

The Lord gifts us another day, wakes us, and lovingly gives us what we need.

Is not every day we breathe miraculous?

Whether you were a boy who drowned with no logical way to survive, or a mother trying to make ends meet for her children.

What's another step into abundance, the miraculous, the unseen, the blessing, the overflowing, and beyond what we could ever imagine?

Not earned by our deeds or efforts—that would make it a wage, not a gift.

A loving gift that our Father wants to give to us, and He has more than we could ever imagine for us.

That is my experience of God and what He has for me, my loved ones, and, I believe, for you—if you're open to receiving it.

Made in the USA
Middletown, DE
02 October 2024

61952941R00060